MW01288654

God is
Loving

God is Loving

A children's book produced by
The Bible Tells Me So Press

Copyright © 2019
The Bible Tells Me So Corporation

All rights reserved. No part of this book, neither text nor illustrations, may be reproduced without permission in writing by the publisher.

PUBLISHED BY
THE BIBLE TELLS ME SO CORPORATION
2111 W. CRESCENT AVE, SUITE C, ANAHEIM, CA 92801
WWW.THEBIBLETELLSMESO.COM

First Printing July, 2019

God loves the
whole world.

He wants us to see

He loves everyone
and each family.

God loves every mom

and
loves
every
dad.

He loves every son

**and daughter
they've had.**

He loves
every child

whatever
    their name;

wherever
they're from

God loves them the same.

Now this includes you,

God loves you for sure,

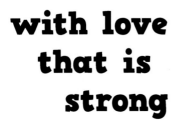

**with love
that is
strong**

and love that is pure.

So through
every day

and every night too,

remember my dear...

God always loves you.

For God
so loved the world...

John 3:16a

For more
books, videos, songs, and crafts
visit us online at
TheBibleTellsMeSo.com

Standing on the Bible and growing!

Made in the USA
Coppell, TX
05 August 2021

60028183R00021